FINDING
GOD
in a LEAF

THE MYSTICISM OF *LAUDATO SI'*

BRIAN GROGAN SJ

A MONTH OF REFLECTIONS

First published in 2018 by Messenger Publications

Cover image: Zamurovic Photography / Shutterstock

ISBN 978 1 78812 004 3

Designed by Messenger Publications Design Department
Typeset in Baskerville & Didot
Printed by W&G Baird Ltd

Messenger Publications,
37 Lower Leeson Street, Dublin D02 W938
www.messenger.ie

DEDICATION

To Elaine, Helen, Phyllis and Marion of
Loving Sister Earth and to all who promote the dream
of universal harmony.

Part Two:
Repair My House!

INTRODUCTION

Luminous Moments

Most people experience moments of delight, awe, wonder or joy in relation to our created world. Unexpectedly, an aspect of nature becomes luminous, as when someone switches on a light in a dark room and you see the colours and shapes of things. Poets and artists live in this dimension much of the time but each of us has a bit of the poet or artist in us, and we occasionally have the kind of experience I am referring to. Patrick Pearse's experiences in 'The Wayfarer' resonate with us:

> Sometimes my heart hath shaken with great joy
> To see a leaping squirrel in a tree,
> Or a red lady-bird upon a stalk,
> Or little rabbits in a field at evening,
> Lit by a slanting sun,
> Or some green hill where shadows drifted by
> Some quiet hill where mountainy man hath sown
> And soon would reap; near to the gate of Heaven;
> Or children with bare feet upon the sands
> Of some ebbed sea, or playing on the streets
> Of little towns in Connacht…

When poets describe such moments, we say 'Yes!' We know what they mean, they speak to our experience and call our attention to something that we would otherwise have missed: they articulate what we cannot express. For me this occurs in the final lines of Wordsworth's 'Ode on the Intimations of Immortality':

> Thanks to the human heart by which we live,
> Thanks to its tenderness, its joys, and fears,

> To me the meanest flower that blows can give
> Thoughts that do often lie too deep for tears.

These moments at which the artist hints are a kind of revelation of what otherwise is hidden. You sense that behind this everyday reality there is something more. So a beautiful sunrise or sunset captivates you, and triggers the awareness that something marvellous is afoot in the heart of things. As Gerard Manley Hopkins puts it in 'God's Grandeur': '…nature is never spent: there lives the dearest freshness, deep-down things'. To experience this brings joy, peace of heart; a sense of the goodness of reality. You feel that you have been privileged. That for no valid reason of which you are aware, a veil has been drawn back for a few moments just for you: you are being invited in.

Mysticism

Invited in to what? Patrick Pearse wrote his poem on the eve of his execution on 3 May 1916, so there is a poignancy about his use of the term 'the gate of heaven'. Wordsworth speaks of 'intimations of immortality'. Both make a connection between the natural and the divine. Joseph Campbell expresses this well: 'When before the beauty of a sunset or a mountain, you pause and exclaim, "Ah," you are participating in divinity.'

Not all poets would say this, of course: religious sensibility influences the interpretation of experience. It is this reference to the divine, however, that we are referring to in speaking of mysticism. The word itself comes from the Greek and means 'hidden' or 'secret', so mysticism has come to refer to the experience of glimpsing what is concealed. Behind the outward presentation of things there lies a richer world than the senses can ordinarily grasp. Those who see behind the mysteries that are presented daily to us – these we can call mystics. Mysticism has come down to earth! To the mystic eye, nothing is boring! The mystic anticipates the awe and delight that we shall all experience at the end but we can all begin to share that fun now.

This is what I am pointing to in writing of the mysticism of *Laudato Si'*: underpinning all its hard facts, analysis and argumentation is a profound view of the mystery of nature itself as revealing the divine. God, Pope Francis affirms, is present in nature, and he wants us to share that perspective, because he believes that it can generate in us a sense of wonder, awe, reverence and love for nature in all its aspects. This sense will make us strong enough to dedicate ourselves to the demanding task of caring for what he calls 'our common home.' When my home is under threat I will fight tooth and nail to protect it and those living in it, because I love it. Such commitment is needed today if our small and fragile planet is to be brought back to health.

Pope Francis asks us to notice the *intimate connection* (234) between God and what is otherwise everyday and ordinary. This is the mystic dimension of reality. Each page in this book will hint at these intimate connections, one for each day of the month. Once you get caught into the deeper mode of seeing the reality that is around you, things are illuminated and become sacred. Your experiences of nature become spiritual experiences; your encounters with others, and especially the poor, become charged with new meaning.

An Enchanted World

For those who are wary of being labelled 'mystic' it may help if we start our journey by noticing that perhaps we all have within us a contemplative streak, a germ of mysticism which may not yet have come to full flower! We started out as infants by being plunged into a world full of surprises and mystery. As a child is reported to have said: 'I was so surprised at being born that I couldn't speak for eighteen months!' We were fascinated by everything: adults, cats, toes, parents' faces, flames and sparks, spoons and prams. All was wonderful and exciting. As children we lived in an enchanted world. Things were not just themselves: there was always something more about them. A mysterious cat used to visit us: it had a life of its own, independent of us. I used to wonder where did it come from and where did it go…?

You may like to revisit that time, to walk again that sacred and unique path along which the world first unfolded for you. I, for instance, used to wonder what clouds could be or what my parents were up to when they knelt to say the Rosary in the evenings. They, after all, were the most important persons in the world, so why were they kneeling to someone else, asking someone for things? And who or where was that someone?

Our school chapel, lit only by the sanctuary lamp, fascinated me by its semi-darkness, as did the priest as he went about his business in a language I could make nothing of. Later, school retreats opened up the life of Jesus and at least for a few days left my soul 'ablaze with God' as St Ignatius says of himself. And I loved the times of silence: something began to go on between myself and a mysterious other, even if I couldn't articulate what it was to which I was being attracted.

Later, theology brought me to a sense of the richness of the Christian faith, and of how amazingly generous are God's dreams for the world. Rudolf Otto's definition of God as 'the mystery which is awesome and fascinating' was helpful: that God, totally other than me, was drawing me irresistibly. The sense of a personal relationship between this God and myself deepened. Martin Buber's book, *I and Thou*, caught me. Pastoral ministry in its innumerable forms gave me a window on how God works on each of our hearts to make us grow in love. But in all this time, while I loved nature, I was reserved about it – and all other earthly beauty! The message was that God was the ultimate goal: and that all this earth would pass away into dust.

Our Secret Beauty

At some point I stumbled on an arresting passage from Thomas Merton:

> In Louisville, at the corner of Fourth and Walnut, in the centre of the shopping district, I was suddenly overwhelmed with the realisation that I loved all those people, that they were mine and I theirs. Then it was as if I suddenly saw the secret beauty of their hearts, the depths of their hearts where neither sin nor desire nor self-knowledge can reach, the core of their reality, the person that each one is in God's eyes. If only they could all see themselves as they really *are*. If only we could see each other that way all the time. There would be no more war, no more hatred, no more cruelty, no more greed…

I found myself yearning for Merton's experience – I felt that to see people as God does would make it a lot easier to love them! The conviction recently expressed by Pope Francis that 'When everything is said and done, we are all infinitely loved' helps me hugely, when I happen to remember it. It's a mystic awareness that people are more than they seem: they are God-connected.

Most recently I have been enthralled by *Laudato Si'* and its insights into the depths of God's presence in creation. It gives me permission to relate with nature in a deeper way without the fear of seeming odd. We all have moments when 'the heart sings unbidden' at the awareness of beauty, when the temporal unveils the eternal. These moments are 'orthodox' rather than out of place and they can glide from passing experiences to extended phases: surely Jesus contemplated the world around him with this consciousness and wishes it for us too?

I now imagine God as an attracting God. God attracts us through the physical world and is luring us home, and drawing creation too into the final scheme of things. So I am back in the 'enchanted world' of childhood which I had abandoned for many years, and the labour of composing these reflections has brought me into a deepening awareness of how the divine is present in everything. Merton highlights this divine presence in a startling way when he says:

> Every moment and every event in every person's life plants something in their soul. For just as the wind carries thousands of winged seeds, so each moment brings with it germs of spiritual vitality that come to rest imperceptibly in people's minds and wills.

You don't have to travel far to encounter God. God is encountering you all the time, trying to enchant you. The germs of spiritual vitality are infectious!

What's Really Going On

We talk easily about what's happening on the surface of our lives. But what's really going on? Beneath the surface level of life on earth lies a strategy, backed by divine power and artistry, that is sweeping everything up into one infinitely complex whole, so that finally God may become all in all. Even to glimpse occasionally that this is what's really going on gives hope, and is an antidote to the view that our common home can never be put to rights, and that human history will end in tragic burnout. We are to live and work in hope, 'with the eyes of our hearts enlightened'. This is what mysticism and contemplation are about.

The insights of science about the cosmos are coming to us thick and fast. Our generation is being showered with insights about the history and structure of creation which were hidden from our predecessors. This new knowledge helps us to understand God's artistic work, appreciate it properly and relate lovingly to its creator. Creation is God's self-revelation, and we have so much to learn from it. Then we can participate more effectively in co-creating and restoring the divine masterpiece.

A Word on Laudato Si'

Pope Francis' encyclical *Laudato Si'* ('May you be praised') was published on June 18, 2015. The title comes from the canticle of St Francis of Assisi composed seven hundred years earlier. As archbishop of Buenos Aires the future pope had paid special attention to the poor of that city. One of his key insights was that what was happening to the poor of the earth is due to the uncontrolled capitalism of the First World. Hence his central theme in *Laudato Si'* is that care for the poor and for the earth are to be an integral dimension of our lives.

Note that in the terms 'nature' and 'creation' we include all that exists, not only what is living and beautiful, but also what is human-made, whether beautiful or not. So God is to be found in computers, in trucks, cars and roads, in soaring buildings and tiny hovels, in steel and in cement, in rubbish-dumps, in stones, and even in weapons of mass destruction. All reality is interconnected within itself and with its maker, so God is hidden in everything.

Finding God in a leaf?

Why choose as a title for these reflections something so humble as a leaf? The answer is that leaves are plentiful, immediately accessible and also wonderful. They speak to us of God; they are a revelation of what God is like and how God works all around us. A single leaf, living or dead, will guide you surely into the mysticism of *Laudato Si'*. So what is a leaf? Leaves are usually thin and flat, with a complex vein system like a network of small canals: these provide for the leaf's tasks a supply of water from the ground. Leaves have pores which take in carbon dioxide, and they maximise their surface area to absorb sunlight as required. This promotes photosynthesis, a complex process which enables the leaf to manufacture nourishing food for the parent plant by a judicious mix of gas, water and light.

Leaves are small but well-organised living factories. Because they are vital to the world as we know it, they have elaborate strategies for dealing with pests and unfavourable seasonal conditions. Leaves look placid and work silently; they have a short life span, but when you meet dead leaves in autumn, salute them with gratitude for all they have achieved. Without them there would be little vegetation and the oxygen vital to life would disappear. And when leaves finally fall to the ground their remaining nutrients are recycled to provide for next year's growth. Nothing of them is wasted; all is given over. They give an instance of that universal self-donating love which, as Dante says, 'moves the sun and the other stars'.

Chat with a Leaf!

Try engaging with an older leaf! The Pope says that 'nature cries out to us' so let's listen to that voice! The dialogue might run as follows: 'Good day! Please tell me your story'. 'Well' says the leaf, 'that big tree beside us is my parent and it gave birth to me this spring. It's been a good life up there: I don't think I ever harmed anyone, and with my 50,000 siblings I helped your species by absorbing CO_2 and providing oxygen. A little while back my parent had to withdraw support of me to conserve itself for winter. So here I am, cracked and crumbling.' 'And what next?' 'Well, like yourself I'll return to dust and become part of something else, a daffodil, perhaps! Receiving and giving back is the rhythm of things. We trees go back some 335 million years – a bit longer than humans, I may say! Someone of your species has said that trees are God's first temples. Not bad! Of course, we all go back to the beginning, so we're the same deep down… But your species destroys so many of us, despite the fact that trees are the earth's lungs, and we could eat up enough CO_2 to save our common home. Can you do anything to help?'

* * * * *

I find that this way of relating to nature offsets my instinct to see material things simply as objects. Try it and enjoy!

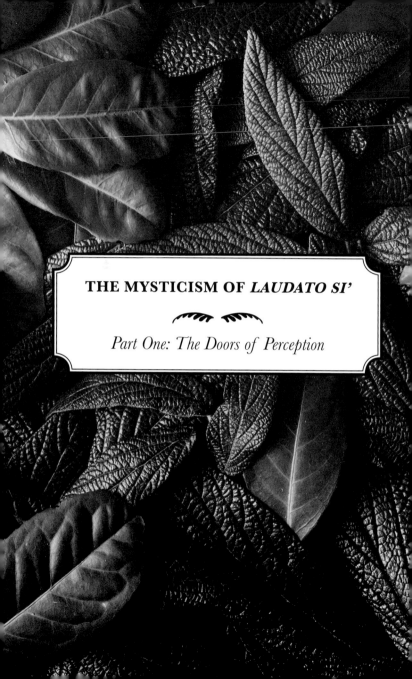

THE MYSTICISM OF *LAUDATO SI'*

Part One: The Doors of Perception

1
Fresh Eyes

Pope Francis' encyclical, *Laudato Si'* on Care for Our Common Home makes painful reading. It challenges us to change our flawed attitudes to the earth, and such change is hard. But behind the tough news is a *mysticism*, a faith-filled or contemplative way of looking at creation with ever-deeper love. In Part One of these pages we will explore first the beauty of creation as hinted at in *Laudato Si'*, then in Part Two the challenges presented to us because of our disfiguring it. The Pope's challenges when read against the backdrop of our new appreciation of the earth's beauty will be charged with new urgency, for when we come to love our earth more deeply, we will be drawn to protect it. The Pope says:

> It is our humble conviction that the divine and the human meet in the slightest detail in the seamless garment of God's creation, in the last speck of dust of our planet (9).

This faith-insight changes everything! Every molecule of creation is sacred. See a plant, a bird, a carrot, a drop of water, a speck of dust in this way and you will begin to see the world as God sees it. Why not start on this exploration now?

Keep coming back to the Pope's statement: take it in as best you can. Share your reflections with others and notice how your heart begins to soften with appreciation and concern for the tiny things of the earth. God is the God of small things, and you meet God in them as well as in the church, the sacraments, the Bible, the Christian community, the poor and in solitary prayer. This is what it means to be contemplative – to see creation with eyes of wonder. Ask St Francis of Assisi and St Ignatius to share with you their way of seeing the world, or recall someone who has already introduced you to the mystery hidden in created things.

The poet William Blake wrote, 'If the doors of perception were cleansed, everything would appear as it is, infinite.' We need to pray for fresh and cleansed eyes, and then, like him we will be able 'to see the world in a grain of sand, and to see heaven in a wild flower, hold infinity in the palm of our hands, and eternity in an hour'.

2
The Caress Of God

The more we come to love nature in all its detail, the more we will want to care for it, because we care for the things we love. Here's the poet D H Lawrence's vision of a single flower – a narcissus – coming into bloom:

> When from a world of mosses and of ferns
> At last the narcissus lifted a tuft of five-pointed stars
> And dangled them in the atmosphere,
> Then every molecule of creation jumped and
> clapped its hands:
> God is born.

St Paul says, 'Creation waits with eager longing' (Rom 8:19). When you next look at a flower, try to imagine the excitement of creation as it achieves its purpose in the perfection of that particular flower. Every molecule does jump and dance because there is no such thing as 'inanimate matter'. St Thomas Aquinas states serenely that all things desire God. They are on the move, striving, though in a different way to us, to realise their potential. Nature has its intentions and achievements. For nature, every day is a birthday, a day of revelation. Watch nature coming alive on a spring morning! The Pope says:

> Each creature has its own purpose. None is superfluous. The entire material universe speaks of God's love, God's boundless affection for us. Soil, water, mountains: everything is, as it were, a caress of God (84).

For the believer, everything in nature is a love-note from God! The real God is not impersonal but rather the great lover who chooses to create in order to convey 'boundless affection' for us. Sky, light, clouds, living things, the delicacy of the flower, the play of the wind on your cheek, these are 'the caresses of God'. God is very close indeed: the big secret is that we walk the world of the divine all the time. Never to be awe-struck is to miss out on the richness of life. Notice some of the caresses of God today!

3

Your Divine Meeting Places

The underlying perspective of *Laudato Si'* is that every molecule of creation is sacred; through each single one God's love is revealed. Creation is God's first self-revelation: it is the work of the Holy Spirit, and so displays God's limitless love and affection for us. It is as if the three divine Persons were saying, 'Let's pull out all the stops so everyone on the face of the earth will be able to see our love. All they'll have to do is to look and they'll see us!' For God, creation is good, both for itself and for our lives. When our impaired vision is corrected we come to see the world as a loving gift, and so are drawn towards God and then towards care of the gift that has been given us. This is the goal of *Laudato Si'*. From this twenty-twenty mystical vision of nature as divine gift, our care for the earth will flow. But because we are small human beings, we need to start somewhere to learn the universal lesson that all is sacred. So the Pope says:

> The history of our friendship with God is always linked to particular places which take on an intensely personal meaning; we all remember places, and revisiting those memories does us much good. Anyone who has grown up in the hills or sat by the spring to drink, or played outdoors in the neighbourhood square, knows that going back to such places gives them a chance to recover something of their true selves (84).

The project Loving Sister Earth, in which I am involved, and which you can access through the internet, endorses this insight and invites you to connect with ancient holy places as a way of gaining energy for the task of caring for contemporary creation. Blessed Henry Newman refers to them as the storehouse of the past and the birthplace of the future. Everywhere in fact is a sacred space but the places hallowed by our ancestors over so many generations are rich in divine associations. Going to such places gives us 'a chance to recover our true selves'. Try doing this and you will notice a sense of connectedness as you return to your roots! As Hopkins says: 'I greet him the days I meet him, and bless when I understand'.

4

The Holy Spirit

A fundamental theme of *Laudato Si'* is the interdependence of all reality, so wherever we stumble on it, we are catching on to the work of the Holy Spirit, whose role is to unify and to facilitate cosmic creativity. We tend to think that the first revelation of the Spirit occurred after Jesus' resurrection but in fact the first Pentecost took place in the great act of creation. There the Spirit of God, brooding over the formless void, gave it shape and meaning. God made us humans come alive by breathing the Spirit of Life into random dust (Gen 2:7). As the Liturgy says, 'The Spirit of God fills the whole world'. We might add, 'and it has always done so!' Our feast of Pentecost highlights the Spirit's creative action in human beings: it calls us into co-creativity with the Spirit in shaping the world. We live in a world reverberating with Spirit, and we are invited to become attuned! The Pope says:

> The Spirit of God has filled the universe with possibilities, and therefore, from the very heart of things, something new can always emerge. The Spirit can be said to possess an infinite creativity (80).

> The Spirit is intimately present at the very heart of the universe, inspiring and bringing new pathways (238).

Hopkins' poem 'God's Grandeur' hints at the Spirit's activity:

> And for all this, nature is never spent;
> There lives the dearest freshness deep down
>   things…
> Because the Holy Ghost over the bent
> World broods with warm breast and with ah!
>   bright wings.

Imagine the Spirit warming the earth as a hen warming her eggs! This gives hope for our battered and disfigured world. Then imagine the Spirit trying to gain entrance into each heart to warm it with love: the Spirit's mission is to 'make us grow in love' and the Spirit is tenacious and indefatigable in achieving that goal. Finally imagine the Spirit trying to find a home in your own heart, so that you may become more alive, more creative, more attuned to the dynamism of our developing cosmos. 'Come, Holy Spirit!'

5

The Precious Book Of Creation

We used to think that spirit and matter were opposed to one another but *Laudato Si'* stresses that the Spirit is active in all matter in order to bring it home to God. Matter is spirit-endowed; it has vast potentiality; it is 'on the move'. Evolution is now widely accepted among Christians as valid, with the added religious dimension that it originates, not of itself, but from the Spirit. The Spirit has been playing in creation for almost fourteen billion years, kneading and moulding it like clay, creating the most beautiful and extraordinary diversity of species. Each of these carries the stamp of life, the mark of the enlivening Spirit. The Pope says:

> God has written a precious book, whose letters are the multitude of created things present in the universe. No creature is excluded from this manifestation of God: from panoramic vistas to the tiniest living form, nature is a constant source of wonder and awe. It is also a continuing revelation of the divine (85).

You can learn to read God's 'precious book' just as you are able to read this little book now! In every detail of nature, God is trying to convey something to you. God wants us never to lose the sense of wonder we had in childhood: 'Children's faces looking up, holding wonder like a cup'. This is to be our adult attitude too. Jesus says: 'Unless you change and become like little children, you will never enter the kingdom of heaven' (Mt 18:3). This mysterious 'kingdom of heaven' is close. It is already given us in nature, and is all around, to be enjoyed, respected and admired. Admire a plant, a bird, or a bee and ask God, 'What are you communicating to me here?' Pierre Teilhard de Chardin, whose insights lie behind *Laudato Si'*, could playfully speak of the clouds in the sky as 'the handwriting of God'. That is the child-mind at work. Try it but not while driving!

6

Mystics In The Making

This is our sixth reflection on the mysticism of *Laudato Si'*. Look back for a few moments on what is happening to your heart as you move along! The theologian Karl Rahner remarked in the 1980s that the Christian of the future will be a mystic or will not be a Christian at all. Are you becoming a mini-mystic by now? It is important that you are, and it is also a thrilling development in you.

The popular image of a mystic is of someone who spends a lot of time alone in solitary prayer, cut off from the distracting world. The mysticism of nature, however, is a gift for everyone in the audience! You may not be a person who spends much time alone with God but as you contemplate nature can you grow in wonder and in awareness that every bit of creation is singing a song to you, and is inviting you to catch on to its melody? Do feelings of awe arise in you as you spend little moments now and then marvelling at what nature keeps coming up with? When you worry about the messiness of life can you envelop it in gratitude for the steadiness of nature's laws of growth? Can you hope that perhaps God hasn't abandoned this chaotic world of ours to its own destructive devices but is creatively at work to bring it to its intended beauty? The Pope says:

> To sense each creature singing the hymn of its existence is to live joyfully in God's love and hope. This contemplation of creation allows us to discover in each thing a teaching which God wishes to hand on to us, since for the believer, to contemplate creation is to hear a message, to listen to a paradoxical and silent voice (85).

To be a mystic, then, you don't have to be a person whose knees are wearing out – though God draws some hearts to that silent intimacy. All you have to do is to look long and lovingly at creation, and let it speak to your heart. Do this for a while today, and you will experience what it is like 'to live joyfully in God's love and hope'. Every garden is a divine schoolroom.

7

Divine Manifestations

We have within us a religious instinct, and if we cultivate it we find ourselves yearning for manifestations of the divine. Hence the interest in angels, apparitions, visions, news of the other world, private revelations and devotions. But where to find God, who often seems absent? *Laudato Si'* suggests: 'Hold it for a moment! You don't need to step away from this world to meet God. God is everywhere in the created world!' Chat up a flower, a fly, a snail, a sunbeam, a shadow, a silhouette, a cloud, the sky and the sea – each is more than just itself. Each of these simple things is a unique manifestation of God, and we are invited to catch on to their revelatory quality. A messy pile of autumn leaves is a divine mystery before being a problem to be swept up! Nightfall is not simply a moment when you have to turn on the light: deeper down it is an invitation to enter into mystery, and there God resides. The Pope says:

> Alongside revelation properly so-called, contained in sacred Scripture, there is a divine manifestation in the blaze of the sun and the fall of night (85).

The Pope here picks out two everyday events that act as bookends for the mystery and wonder which are crammed into our waking hours: dawn and dusk. Sunrise and sunset – whenever we are lucky to see them – can evoke a sense of the wonder of their creator. They can inspire silent adoration in us, for the word 'adoration' means 'putting your hand to your mouth', and we instinctively put our hands to our mouths when we encounter something mysterious or wonderful. Every time we catch on to the beauty of a person or thing, we are experiencing a moment of revelation. Our days overflow with little revelations of the divine, so let's not allow them to pass unnoticed. Such quiet revelations interrupt our prosaic ways of thinking, and open us up to something deeper. As the beholders of the divine display, we catch on and 'adore', for God is truly present in these moments, even if in a humbler way than in the Eucharist. It is not accidental that across the globe people choose to pray at dawn and at dusk, when nature is often showing off her splendour in the nicest possible way.

8

An Attracting God

A lecturer once devastated me by asserting that mysticism 'is all mist and schism!' 'Stick to meditation!' he thundered, 'don't let your heart get lost in the clouds.' He would have no dabbling in nature mysticism: it led, he said, to pantheism. Had he come across something mysterious he would have attacked or domesticated it immediately. He needed everything to be clear and certain, and was ill at ease with the notion that God is full of surprises. I hope he has adjusted by now, for he died some years ago!

Mysticism is an umbrella word for the human experience that in creation the divine is close, beckoning, welcoming, loving and accessible. Nature includes humans as well as humpbacked whales, warblers and wall-flowers. Around us there are 7.4 billion persons, each of them images of God, however disguised or disfigured. God wishes to be found in each, especially in the poor. So the Pope says:

> There is a mystical meaning to be found in a leaf, in a mountain trail, in a dewdrop, in a poor person's face (233). The mystic experiences the intimate connection between God and all things (234).

To experience the intimate connection between God and things, we can, as a simple exercise, take one small leaf and stay with it until we catch on to its connectedness with the one who made and sustains it.

God wants to be found not only in cells, caves and chapels but also in nature, and in the chaos of human history. We are invited into divine company to sit with God and see the world from that privileged vantage point! We live in the presence of an attracting God, who is constantly trying to get our attention. Through every crumb of creation this God is leading us ever onward and inward to the heart of things, to God's very self. God is luring us on from in front rather than urging us from behind. The world may be in serious trouble but divine energy is not running down: it is attracting the cosmos to the one who, having made it, will complete it in ways beyond our wildest imagining.

9

The Divine Womb

Towards the end of *Laudato Si'* there is a magnificent paragraph, all too short, on the Eucharist. Every line is rich, and we will unfold its meaning over the next few reflections. The theologian von Balthasar says, 'the cosmos is the monstrance of God'. Pope Francis says, however, that nature is not simply an outer frame for the sacred but is itself sacred and reveals the divine. Then comes a daring statement:

Jesus comes, not from above, but from within (236).

Alarm bells may ring at the idea that Jesus does *not* come 'from above'. Like me, you may have been brought up with the sandwich image of the world: heaven above, hell below and earth in the middle. That is how the ancients thought: the gospels speak of Jesus coming to us 'from on high' and 'ascending into heaven' as he goes away. This gives the impression of a celestial visitor who belongs to another world than ours. The sandwich model, however, was simply a scaffolding to help build the great theological truth that Jesus is divine, that he comes from God. Scaffoldings can change but the building remains firm.

In saying that Jesus comes from within the Pope is employing a model better suited to what we now know of the interconnectedness of everything. So instead of a sandwich, imagine all reality perhaps as a great web, a womb or a balloon! Einstein used the image of a mollusc to describe reality. Some such image underlies St Paul's statement, 'In God we live and move and have our being' (Acts 17:28). Everything exists in the womb of divine being! God is at the heart of all reality, which includes past, present and future, matter and spirit and all human history. We ourselves are there and are connected with our deceased family and friends, now fully alive. The divine web or womb or balloon includes Jesus: he emerges into our world not from some 'outer space' but from within this divine reality, as we do. So we can find him in this world of ours. He is divine but not an alien: he is like his brothers and sisters in all things. This dramatically deepens our appreciation of nature!

10
Finding God In Our World

Continuing from the previous reflection, we note first the Christian belief that Jesus comes from God: he is divine. 'God from God, Light from Light, True God from True God' – so says the Creed. With that truth always firmly in place we can explore further the surprising statement that Jesus comes to us from within creation. The Pope says:

> He comes from within, that we might find him in this world of ours (236).

Think of a daffodil bulb planted in late autumn. It doesn't look anything spectacular, and it lies passive in cold and dark soil until springtime. Then it begins to unfold according to its own mysterious laws of growth. At the right time it blossoms in all its glory. That blossom has always been in the bulb potentially, but time must pass and conditions must be right for it to become what it is destined to be. To achieve its goal it uses the materials which are to hand – soil, nutrition, water, sunlight.

Now just as the daffodil blossom was hidden by God in creation from the beginning, we can think also of Jesus as hidden in creation by God from the very start. All of us indeed were there at the beginning, for we are all made from the original cosmic stardust. The gospel genealogies of Jesus are irrelevant if we think of Jesus as being introduced into our human story from outside the cosmos and at the last moment.

They are in fact hinting at how Jesus' family tree is rooted in the origin of things. They remind us how, generation after generation, each human conception inched his story forward. Not that those involved knew or cared about the outcome, but God did. God's very self would eventually emerge, because it was there from the start. This is the mystery woven into creation and Jesus carried its hope from the very beginning. He is the flower that burst into bloom 2000 years ago, and now remains forever with us. To the contemplative eye, this everyday material world of ours is always serving divine purposes: we can let ourselves be touched by 'awesome wonder' at God's residence 'in this world of ours' since the world's foundation.

11
Deep Incarnation

Scripture scholars use terms like 'deep incarnation' to jolt us into the insight that Jesus' roots are not on the surface level of our world but are embedded in the earth which began so long ago. St John does not say that the Word was made *man* or was made *human*; he goes deeper and says that the Word was made *flesh*. Flesh, in Scripture, means 'all that is created'. Impelled by the Spirit, matter evolved so that at the right moment, Jesus emerged as a child of the earth, 'one of the children of the year'. The gospels emphasise that Mary's child is uniquely 'of the Holy Spirit' because in him the goal of creation is first and best realised. What is said of Jesus refers to us too: as his siblings we all share in his 'success story'. We are destined for divinisation. Deep incarnation also implies the divinisation of the material world in which we are embedded.

We can imagine matter quivering with excitement as it played its part, molecule by molecule, in the long history of

Jesus' coming-to-be. Hopkins catches this energy: 'The earth is *charged* with the grandeur of God'. Think of an electrical charge pulsing through matter, and you are not far from what physicists say about the liveliness and potentiality of matter. As part of earth, you are 'charged' and enlivened whenever you encounter God. The Pope says:

> The destiny of all creation is bound up with the mystery of Christ (99).

So to find God we do not have to look outside the cosmos, but within. Jesus is Emmanuel; 'God-with-us'. He is the quickening element in this world of ours, at levels that we can only guess at. He is far more with us than we with him. He was already present in every aspect of creation from the beginning. Creation came to consciousness after billions of years, and then, just very recently, Jesus emerged, the definitive presence of the divine, the fulfilment of all that had gone before, and the promise of what is still to come. Through his resurrection, everything is already rising and is directed to its fulfilment when God will be all in all. Then the divine will suffuse all of creation, like the glow of a perfect dawn. Deep resurrection is the destiny of the cosmos. No wonder creation can clap its hands and look forward to sharing in the glory and freedom of the children of God! (Rom 8:21)

12
The Eucharist

The Eucharist is embedded in cosmic history: it stretches all the way back to the Big Bang 13.8 billion years ago and also points forward to the divinisation of all things, to the great cosmic banquet, when creator and creation will rejoice together. So the Pope can say:

> The Eucharist joins heaven and earth; it embraces and penetrates all creation. In the bread of the Eucharist, creation is projected towards divinisation, towards the holy wedding feast, towards unification with the Creator himself (236).

Carl Sagan offers a homely image which can help us catch on to this vision. He says that if you wish to make an apple pie from scratch, you must first invent the universe. Can this be true? Well, a pie needs flour, and if you make your own flour from scratch, you'll need wheat and milling equipment. To get that, you'll need farms and metal, soil and minerals and farming skills. You'll need seeds, of course. Likewise for the apples – and don't forget some bees for the pollination work! You'll need to organise the climate, else nothing will grow. So throw in the sun, clouds, rain and seasons. Invent electricity, add water and a few cloves and sugar to taste. To truly say 'it was I who made that pie!' you'll have to make the primary elements, which you'd sweep up from dead stars. And don't forget to create a dynamic order so everything happens at the right time and dovetails with everything else.

Now give yourself some space, perhaps with others, to imagine what has to go into the making of the ingredients of the Eucharist. How true it is to say that it embraces all creation. We are the first generation that knows at least in outline the long and complex history of matter: that makes us hugely privileged. The veil has been pulled back in our lifetime so that we can reverence and adore the mystery of what God is quietly up to. In the Eucharist, the simplest things, bread and wine, are transformed into the divine. The ears of wheat and the grapes used at the Last Supper do not stand alone: they represent all creation, and in the Eucharist it is 'our world' that is being transfigured. God is very close indeed. A smile of appreciation for being given a glimpse of the divine imagination at work in the Eucharist is surely in order!

13
Divinisation

At the Offertory of the Eucharist, the priest puts a drop of wine into the chalice and says quietly, 'May we become sharers in the divinity of Christ, who humbled himself to share our humanity'. What a statement this is, to affirm that we are sharers in Christ's divinity! An outsider at the back of the church might expect a cheer from the congregation or at least a heartfelt 'amen'. Yet, there is no response: Mass goes steadily on. The Western Church makes little of divinisation, whereas it is a rich theme in the Eastern Church. The Pope says:

> In the bread of the Eucharist, Creation is projected towards divinisation (236).

To catch on to this, we need to think outside the box, because while God is not limited by any boundaries, we are! Do you think that humankind reached its peak with the arrival of *homo sapiens*? When Bronowski wrote *The Ascent of Man*, why did he stop with us as we now are? Who are we to decide the cut-off point of human possibility? Does God smile at our narrowness of imagination? Is C S Lewis right in asserting that with the emergence of Jesus in the world a radical leap in human evolution took place? If some of us began sprouting wings the whole world would pay attention and say, 'perhaps we are beginning to fly'! But could it be that through the action of Jesus we are beginning to be transformed to the level of the divine?

With the incarnation of God in Jesus, what has begun is the development of the human to the divine dimension. When evolutionary developments happen, certain factors become favoured over others: in this instance the relevant shift is not on the level of physique or of intelligence, but on the level of spirit and consciousness. This development enables us to 'become sharers in the divinity of Christ'. The pages of the gospels rustle with the 'Good News' that we are being changed from the inside out; that our capacity for the divine is secretly being realised, that we are becoming the children of God and are being elevated to meet God face to face – as friends. We live in a world of potential gods and goddesses, and the cosmos itself is 'projected towards divinisation'! See your fellow-travellers in a plane or bus in this light.

14
Summary

At the end of this part of the book, it may help to gather some of the 'mystical' passages in *Laudato Si'*. Taken together they can suitably overwhelm you!

> The divine and the human meet in the slightest detail
> in the seamless garment of God's creation, in the last
> speck of dust of our planet (9).
> Each creature has its own purpose. None is

superfluous. The entire material universe speaks of God's love, God's boundless affection for us. Soil, water, mountains: everything is a caress of God (84). God has written a precious book, whose letters are the multitude of created things. From panoramic vistas to the tiniest living form, nature is a constant source of wonder and awe. It is also a continuing revelation of the divine. Alongside revelation in sacred Scripture, there is a divine manifestation in the blaze of the sun and the fall of night (85).

The sun and the moon, the cedar and the little flower, the eagle and the sparrow – no creature is self-sufficient. Creatures exist only in dependence on each other, in the service of each other (86).

The universe unfolds in God, who fills it completely. Hence, there is a mystical meaning to be found in a leaf, in a mountain trail, in a dewdrop, in a poor person's face (233). Standing awestruck before a mountain, we cannot separate this experience from God (234).

There is a subtle mystery in each of the movements and sounds of this world. The perceptive will capture what is being said when the wind blows, the trees sway, water flows, flies buzz, doors creak, birds sing or in the sound of strings or flutes, the sighs of the sick, the groans of the afflicted... (note 159).

Stop here for a moment. Look! Let a tiny aspect of nature come into focus. Admire. Fall in love. Notice peace and joy within you. Sense the mystery. When enriched, move on, only to return later. Gradually the doors of your perception will be cleansed: you see beyond, and glimpse the divine.

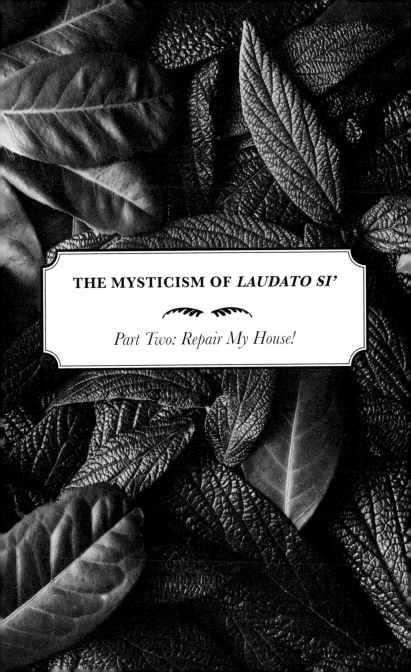

THE MYSTICISM OF *LAUDATO SI'*

Part Two: Repair My House!

Loving Stewardship

Now that our reflections on the rich mysticism which underpins *Laudato Si'* have cleansed 'the doors of our perception' we turn to the wretched plight of sister earth and allow an emotional response to well up in our hearts. Such a response, the Pope says, is not naive romanticism, for it affects our choices. The Pope says:

> If we approach nature without this openness to awe and wonder, if we no longer speak the language of fraternity in our relationship with the world, our attitude will be that of ruthless exploiters... But if we feel intimately united with all that exists, then care will well up spontaneously in us (11).
>
> Responsible care of creation is an essential part of the Christian faith (64).

Later he adds:

> The Eucharist is a source of light and motivation for our concerns for the environment, directing us to be stewards of all creation (236).

What we love, we defend and care for. Now that we have seen how the Eucharist embodies Christ and all of creation, we become more gentle and respectful of all that exists. We are to imitate God's own loving kindness and providence in our care for planet earth.

Pope Francis opts firmly for the image of the stewardship of creation (Gen 2:7): we are to till and keep the garden of God, to dress it in beauty. He rejects the image of 'dominion' (Gen 1:28) which infers that nature's role is simply to serve human interests, after which it can be discarded as useless rubbish. To the eyes of a mystic, that is, to a contemplative person who sees as God sees, nothing that God has made can be called rubbish.

We sit at the table of divine generosity, surrounded by all our fellow-species. They gaze on us with troubled eyes, fearful that we will continue to wipe them out. One after another they ask us, 'must you obliterate me?' What do we say? 'Even the fleeting life of the least of beings is the object of God's love, and in its few seconds of existence, God enfolds it with his affection' (77). As stewards we are to do as God does and to enfold all things with affection, protect them and praise God for the wonder of their being.

16
Our Common Home

It is worthwhile to explore the riches of the Pope's chosen term for mother earth – our common home. The word 'home' stirs up in us a world of memories and emotions. If you have had a happy childhood, home is the place for which you feel the greatest affection: it blended good relationships with the particularities of the place where you began your life. As Elvis Presley has it, home is where the heart is. This resonates with the saying, 'It takes hands to build a house, but only hearts can build a home'. The Pope says:

> Our common home is like a sister with whom we share our life, and a beautiful mother who opens her arms to embrace us (1).

It is hard to imagine a more heart-stirring name for the world than 'our common home'. 'Our planet is a homeland and humanity is one people living in a common home' (164). We must rediscover what our ancestors enjoyed – a deep and loving sense of relationship with planet earth and all its inhabitants. As children we shared what was perhaps a small home; now we share a planet, and like St Francis of Assisi of old we in our time are charged with the task of protecting and repairing it.

Never have we so hurt and mistreated our common home as we have in the last two hundred years. Yet we are called to be instruments of God our Father, so that our planet might be what he desired when he created it a haven of peace, beauty and fullness (53).

It's all about renewing relationships – with other members of the human family, but with the wider non-human family too, so that earth may become 'home, sweet home' to all its inhabitants.

The ultimate purpose of other creatures is not to be found in us. Rather, with us and through us, all creatures are moving towards a common point of arrival, which is God, where the risen Christ embraces and illumines all things. We are called to lead all creatures back to their creator (83).

Even now we are journeying towards our common home in heaven. We come together to take charge of this home which has been entrusted to us, knowing that all the good which exists here will be taken up into the heavenly feast (243).

Together we are entrusted by God with this work. The labour of collaboration begets community among us, and that is already a blessing even if our work seems to show little fruit otherwise. Community in our home is God's intention.

Mysticism With Open Eyes

We enter here into the painful side of mysticism. Genuine mystics are moved by what they see, whether it be painful or pleasant. To contemplate is to take 'a long, loving look at the real' whether the real is beautiful or disfigured. The mystic tries to find God not only in what is radiant and lovely but in the distortion of all which God made good. God was in disguise in the passion of Jesus and is likewise in the contemporary passion of sister earth.

To catch this dimension theologian J B Metz coined the striking phrase, 'mysticism with open eyes'. An enlisted German teenager during the Second World War, he was reacting to the fact that the eyes of many good Christians were closed to the reality of the Holocaust. God, he believed, was there – only not in attractive form but in agony, but people were not present to this aspect of the divine. He lamented the absence of prophetic voices who would scream in protest at the genocide that was grinding systematically on. How, he wondered, might wooden doctrines and practices be transformed so that believers could pour out mercy on a suffering world and bind up the wounds of a savage passage of history?

His generation has passed but today our situation is not dissimilar. The Pope says:

> Our sister (earth) now cries out to us because of the
> harm we have inflicted on her (2).

We cannot stand idly by while nature suffers. We must shift from a culture of indifference to engagement. Mysticism with open eyes begets deep feeling for suffering of whatever kind. An integral ecology is needed, made up of simple daily gestures which break with the logic of violence, exploitation and selfishness. Such gestures are demanding but they also possess a hidden joy; they bring our lives back into harmony with the gracious dynamics of nature, where God is present. I keep on my desk a small snail-shell as a reminder of all the species that took millions of years to make but have disappeared from earth. Perhaps Noah should be made the patron saint of those who fight for the survival of the species that yet remain.

18

Healing A Sick Planet

The sickness of planet earth leads to the sickness of its inhabitants, and especially the poor. The Pope says:

> The violence present in our hearts, wounded by sin, is reflected in the symptoms of sickness evident in the soil, the water, the air, and in all forms of life (2).

> The earth, our home, is beginning to look more and more like an immense pile of filth (21).

> We need only take a frank look at the facts to see that our common home is falling into serious disrepair (61).

Global warming brings many casualties, especially to women, to the marginal poor and the eco-system. It leads to poverty and forced migration, which are breeding grounds for human trafficking, forced labour, prostitution and even organ trafficking. Hence the Pope says:

> Concern for the environment needs to be joined to a sincere love for our fellow human beings and an unwavering commitment to resolving the problems of society (91).

A mysticism of open eyes leads to a mysticism of helping hands. A healthy mysticism must express itself in resistance to evil. 'No one' says Dorothy Day 'has a right to sit down and feel hopeless about the world: there is too much to do. No one has to do everything, but everyone has to do something.'

We can turn the sordid ravaging of nature into occasions for loving action, compassion and action for justice. And we can pray.

> We can make gestures of loving generosity (58).
> Hope would have us recognise that there is always a way out (61).
> We must not think that our efforts are not going to change the world. They benefit society, often unbeknown to us, for they call forth a goodness which, though unseen, inevitably tends to spread (212).

Mysticism focuses on the present, not the long-range future. We do not know how human history will close or whether we will succeed in saving the planet from a major ecological disaster. What we can do is to influence the present: we are commissioned to do this and we are changed for the better in the doing.

19

Oceans

Seas and oceans cover seventy per cent of the surface of the globe. They offer us a rich world for contemplation in their varied moods, in the steady ebb and flow of the tides, in the play of sunlight and moonlight, in the power of wind and storm. As a child I remember that when my father was upset or in a dark mood he would walk four miles to the coast and spend time contemplating the sea, then return home a different man. Think back to the time you saw the sea for the first time. Watch small children on the beach and recover your experience of awe and delight at something so wonderful and strange. The seas are also home to eighty per cent of all life on earth. That life began in the oceans which nurtured it until it was ready to step ashore. We and all living things have seventy per cent water in our make-up. If earth is our mother, the seas are as a grand-mother to us!

Because they cannot be tamed, the seas give us a feeling that we are faced with formidable power, charming but also threatening. But in Hebrew understanding the sea is a creature subject to divine command. Yahweh dries up the Red Sea to create a safe path for his people as they flee from Egypt. Jesus' power to calm the Sea of Galilee and to walk on its waves hints at his divinity. God's power over the sea symbolises divine mastery over the storms of human history, and in the closing book of the New Testament a sea of crystal symbolises the luminous peace of a renewed universe.

But each of the five great oceans bears a toxic wound – a vast island made of floating plastic, which generates a 'plastic soup' that is finding its way into marine life and thus into the food chain. The plastic we throw away is coming back to haunt us. Many coral reefs are already barren.

The Pope asks:

> Who turned the wonder-world of the seas into underwater cemeteries bereft of colour and life?' (41).

He argues that the oceans need to be made part of our 'global commons' (174). So, contemplate the sea; allow yourself to be moved by its beauty, power and restless energy. Then grieve for the oceans of the world, support marine conservation groups and pray that the destruction of so precious a resource may soon be reversed.

20
Water

Contemplate the rivers, streams, wells and all sources of fresh water, including the rain and the kitchen tap! Fall in love with water, and then make a commitment to do what you can to protect it.

The Pope has much to say about our care for water.

One particularly serious problem is the poor quality of water available to one billion of the world's poor. Unsafe water results in deaths and the spread of water-related diseases caused by micro-organisms and chemical substances. Dysentery and cholera cause infant mortality. Underground water sources are threatened by the pollution produced by mining, farming and industry. Detergents and chemical products pour into our rivers, lakes and seas (29).

Even as the quality of available water is constantly diminishing, there is a growing effort to privatise it, so it becomes a commodity subject to market laws. Yet access to safe and free drinkable water is a basic and universal human right: without it the poor are denied the right to a life consistent with their inalienable dignity (30).

Scarcity of water increases the cost of food. An acute water shortage may occur within a few decades. While the environmental repercussions could affect billions of people, the control of water by multinationals may soon become a major source of conflict. Again the poor will suffer most (31).

The waters of the world are interlinked, and there is a limited amount of water on the planet. Each of us uses it, so each is challenged to conserve it and to promote its sustainable use. As the Pope said recently, 'the right to water is decisive for the future of humanity, and I ask myself if we are not moving toward a great world war over water'. He added that while the situation is urgent, it is not insurmountable. 'Our commitment to giving water its proper place calls for developing a culture of care – that may sound poetic, but that is fine because creation is a poem.'

With St Francis of Assisi we can praise the creator for the gift of water:

> Praised be you, my Lord, through Sister Water,
> who is very useful and humble and precious and chaste (87).

21
The World From Within

Economics and politics make us look at the world as if we were superior to it. We can spend much time spectating things as if they meant little or nothing to us. But as minor mystics, we try to gaze on created reality from the divine perspective. The Pope asks us to become more conscious of our bondedness with all beings: we all started out together, and while we are indeed distinct now, we are tightly interwoven on planet earth. We are joined in a splendid universal communion, the dance of the species, and that dance will endure forever, for we have a common destiny, the transfigured glory of our common home, where all creation will rejoice together. The Pope says:

> As believers, we do not look at the world from without but from within, conscious of the bonds with which the Father links us to all beings (216).
> Living our vocation to be protectors of God's handiwork is essential to a life of virtue; it is not an optional aspect of our Christian experience (217).

This spirituality, nourished by the truths that science unfolds about the cosmos, can motivate us to passionate concern for the protection of our world. An authentic spirituality cannot be otherworldly and remote from human concerns. We cannot live piously as if the Incarnation had never happened. We need an ecological conversion, whereby the effects of our encounter with Jesus Christ become evident in our caring relationship with the world around us.

We are to join with Jesus in his way of seeing the world. For him not one bird is forgotten before God (Lk 12:6). He has taken to himself this material world and is now intimately present to each being, surrounding it with his affection and penetrating it with his light (77). How then can we possibly mistreat creatures or cause them harm? We are to be caring mystics, living out our lives with sensitivity and love for all our fellow-creatures.

22
Gardens

Gardens offer endless scope for budding mystics! They are safe places, full of life, abounding in beauty. Where there is a garden, there will be water and living things with their varied beauty. Charles Darwin, although remembered as the great proponent of evolution, saw himself primarily as a beholder of the natural world. He spent much of his life contemplating the simplest things, and he ends his great work, *The Origin of Species*, by noting: 'It is interesting to contemplate an entangled bank...' This humble bank is clothed with many plants, with birds singing, insects flitting about and worms crawling through the damp earth. It leads him to reflect that 'these elaborately constructed forms, so different from each other and dependent on each other… have all been produced by laws acting around us.'

So, find your entangled bank, contemplate it, muse on its long history and reflect on what it is trying to say to you. Let this be your holy place where you fall in love with the natural world and with its maker. Let the tapestry of life come alive under your gaze. Perhaps you may exclaim, like Darwin, 'It has been for me a glorious day, like giving to a blind man eyes.' The Pope says:

> The biblical texts tell us to 'till and keep' the garden
> of the world (cf Gen 2:15). 'Tilling' refers to culti-
> vating, ploughing or working, while 'keeping' means
> caring, protecting, overseeing and preserving (67).

Gardens are important in Scripture, and in the Bible they offer revelations for our ecologically-endangered times. Eden is described in all its beauty: God pulls out all the stops for humankind, and walks there in the cool of the evening, hoping to meet with Adam and Eve. This garden – *paradise* in Greek – is given into their care but they soon mismanage it by plucking fruit from the tree of knowledge of good and evil. In this sense we might say that our 'original sin' is to spoil the handiwork of God in nature. But it was in a garden that Mary of Magdala met her risen Lord in the disguise of a gardener, and our ruptured relationship iwa radically healed. The Lord still walks in our earth garden and wishes to encounter us there, so out you go!

A Civilisation Of Love

A civilisation of love is everyone's dream. It is also the dream of God. It was the dream of Jesus, who commanded us to love one another as he loves us. It is the task of the Holy Spirit – with our participation – to bring about this civilisation of love. God's dream cannot be otherwise, since God is love, and all relationships emanating from God are relationships of love.

We are invited to enter into the divine vision of a world in harmony, where everyone is at home with one another, where all feel wanted and included, where everything is shared and each rejoices in the uniqueness of those around them. This vision would transfigure economics, politics, social life. But it demands that we move way beyond personal concerns. 'This pool of private charity must flow as a world-embracing sea.' Like God, we are to be committed to the common good, we are to be resolute in our care for our neighbours and our planet, even at personal cost. We live as one family in a common home, of which both the members and the contents are entrusted to us by God. This is *Laudato Si's* mystical way of seeing the world. There is a generosity all around us: we are caught into 'a universal fraternity that inspires us to love and accept the wind, the sun and the clouds' (228). 'Nature herself is filled with words of love' (224). We are to reciprocate that love. The Pope says:

> The Church sets before the world the ideal of a civilisation of love. Love in social life – political, economic and cultural – must become the constant and highest norm for all activity. Love, overflowing with small gestures of mutual care, is civic and

political, and it makes itself felt in every action that seeks to build a better world (231).

Blake says, 'we are put on earth a little space / that we may learn to bear the beams of love'. We are indeed to learn the intensity of God's love as revealed in creation but also to bear witness to the other 'beams of love', namely, those which demand self-sacrificing love.

Social love moves us to devise strategies to halt environmental degradation and to encourage a culture of care which would permeate all of society. This requires an engaged spirituality. When we join God in this project, and live out of self-donating love, deep joy can flood our hearts, and this is a sharing in nothing less than divine joy.

24
The Passion Of Sister Earth Today (1)

The Foot Washing

Lord, what went on in your passion touches all time and space, all matter and every person. So let me now learn to link your passion with the present passion of humankind and of creation, so that Easter joy may dawn upon us all. After washing the feet of the disciples, you said, 'I have set you an example; do as I have done'. But what can I do now to ease the world's pain? The Pope says:

> The Creator does not abandon us; he never forsakes his loving plan. Humanity still has the ability to work together in building our common home. Particular appreciation is owed to those who tirelessly seek to resolve the tragic effects of environmental degradation on the lives of the world's poorest (13).

Lord, I can serve at least one needy person, protect some

corner of the earth. Let me do so, in companionship with you.'

The Garden

Dear Lord, let me spend time with you in the Garden of Gethsemane. There you endured the agony of the world. Help me to endure with a loving eye the agony today of the garden of nature entrusted to our care. The Pope says:

> The earth, our home, is beginning to look more and more like an immense pile of filth (21).
> Who turned the wonder-world of the seas into underwater cemeteries bereft of colour and life? (41).

Let my distress translate into loving action against local garbage.

The Arrest

Lord, soldiers came and dragged you off to the authorities. We in our times take nature by force and betray her kindness to us. The Pope says:

> Our Sister, Mother Earth, now cries out to us because of the harm we have inflicted on her by our abuse of the goods with which God has endowed her. Our violence is reflected in the sickness of soil, water, air and in all forms of life (2).

Let me never again abuse the kindness of nature.

The Crowning with Thorns

Dear Lord, innocent though you were, you were scourged, mocked, forced to wear a crown of thorns. I find people forced to wear crowns of thorns today--children whose eyes are without tears, without dreams, as they starve to death in the arms of their helpless parents. Pope Francis says:

> We fail to see that some people are mired in desperate poverty, with no way out, while others have not the

faintest idea of what to do with their possessions…
These consider themselves more human than others,
as if born with greater rights (90).

Teach me to respect and love the despised and to serve them in whatever ways I can.

25
The Passion Of Sister Earth Today (2)

The Sorrowful Way

Dear Lord, a few brave people tried to comfort you in your Passion – your Mother and other women, Simon from Cyrene… Would I have risked being with them? The Pope says:

> Injustices abound and growing numbers of people are deprived of basic human rights and considered expendable… This is a summons to solidarity and a preferential option for the poorest of our brothers and sisters (158).

Let me protest on behalf of those who are being cruelly treated.

The Crucifixion

Lord, I gaze on you as you hang on your Cross. Teach me how I can help to take even one person down from their cross today. The Pope says:

> Food thrown out is stolen from the table of the poor (50).

> Purchasing is always a moral act, not simply an economic one *(206)*.

I can start here!'

The Vigil at the Tomb

Lord, it is Holy Saturday, and all is over. My soul is numb, but let me take my stance with Mary who still cares for us and our world. As a good mother, she keeps vigil and doesn't know what it means to give up. The Pope says:

> Mary now cares with maternal affection and pain for this wounded world. Just as her pierced heart mourned the death of Jesus, so now she grieves for the sufferings of the crucified poor and for the creatures we have laid waste (241).

Let me keep vigil with her and intercede for all who kill our sources of life.

The Resurrection

Dear Lord, Easter has arrived, with its message of lasting hope and joy. Glory is our destiny in a transfigured creation, where weeping and mourning will be ended forever and all creation will be reconciled. The Pope says:

> Mary, completely transfigured, now lives with Jesus. In her glorified body part of creation has reached the fullness of its beauty. She now understands the meaning of all things (241).

I ask her to share with me 'the meaning of all things' so that I may learn that no speck of creation is meaningless. May I work for your world in the hope that you will make all things new and restore to even greater beauty the masterpiece of creation which we have disfigured.

My Neighbour's Hidden Glory

In the introduction I quoted a mystic moment of Thomas Merton, when he saw the people in the shopping mall as they really are, the person each one is in God's sight. Such moments can come our way too, when the doors of perception are cleansed. There is a rich depth waiting to be discovered in everyone around us. We can be explorers, and then heralds of this truth. The Pope says:

> Authentic human development has a moral character. It presumes full respect for the human person (2).
>
> A mystical and contemplative relatedness knows how to see the sacred grandeur of our neighbour (*The Joy of the Gospel*, 92).

In many passages of Scripture God reveals to us who we really are. We are told that when we were small God loved us with everlasting love: that our names are written on the palms of God's hands; that we are made little less than the angels, and that the divine plans for us are plans for peace and not disaster: there is a future full of hope in store for us. We are the beloveds, the friends of God. We are to abide in that love and not be afraid or let our hearts be troubled: in the valley of darkness God is with us to bring us comfort; at the close of our lives God will come to us and take us home, so that where God is, we may also be. God will not call to mind our sins, but welcome us, crown us with glory and say, 'Well done, good and faithful servant; enter into my joy!'

Don't blame God after all this if you still think little of yourself – or of someone else! Ask for the cleansing of your perception so that you may see with Pope Francis that when everything is said and done, you – and they – are infinitely loved. This will make you more sensitive to the limitless dignity of everyone, especially the despised and the poor, and also those you dislike. As Merton says, 'If only they could all see themselves as they really are. If only we could see each other that way all the time. There would be no more war, no more hatred, no more cruelty, no more greed.' Pray to share in this grace!

27

The Magnificence Of God

In their search for solutions to climate change most commentators simply leave God out of the picture. Scientists tend to brush aside the God-question: 'God is dead, or at best distant, ineffectual, irrelevant: meanwhile there is urgent work to be done'. But *Laudato Si'* refers to God one hundred and seventy-eight times: what portrait emerges?

In her novel, *Eat, Pray, Love*, Liz Gilbert is asked what sort of God she believes in. 'A magnificent God!' is her answer. And this is the image of God portrayed in *Laudato Si'*. There is no apology for introducing God, no wading through philosophical arguments to justify God's existence. God simply IS, and is presented as compelling and overarching. The God of *Laudato Si'* has a comprehensive and breathtaking project for the cosmos, and can achieve that project, for to God all creation belongs, and so to God all things are possible. This God is not distant but immeasurably close to us, close to every atom, every moment, every event of our world. God enfolds every least thing with affection, for divine love brims over and covers the earth. All is sacred.

God is the electrifying, surging, loving energy within everything. The cosmos is a divine love-song: if the singer were to stop, nothing would remain but silence. We are caught into this lavish cascade of imaginative loving, and are meant to sing its melody. The God of *Laudato Si'* is a trusting God, who provides us with a common home and calls us to help to care for it. Ecological conversion for us means that with God's help we foster universal harmony between God, humankind and creation. The poor of the earth are God's special concern and must be ours also.

We are not threatened with punishment for our ravaging of the divine handiwork but are challenged radically to reform our lives and collaborate with God in restoring the world to its intended beauty. There is hope for the restoration of all things. The Pope says:

> At the end, we will find ourselves face to face with the infinite beauty of God (243).

God is even now bringing about the divinisation of the world and drawing reality home (236). At the end God will be all in all, and a transfigured cosmos will sing *Laudato Si'*, 'May You be praised'.

28
What Ought I Do?

The Ignatian review of consciousness or *examen* can help convert us to care for creation and for the most vulnerable of the human family. The Pope is unequivocal:

> Living our vocation to be protectors of God's handiwork is essential to a life of virtue; it is not an optional or a secondary aspect of our Christian experience (217).

So I find a quiet place to meet the Lord: I sit with him and quietly gaze in on the world as an astronaut would. He is 'present to everyone and everything' (226). So we can chat as friend to friend.

Be Grateful

We were conceived in the heart of God, and for this reason 'each of us is the result of a thought of God. Each of us is willed, each of us is loved, each of us is necessary' (65).

God has entrusted part of the world to me (5).

I am called to be an instrument of our Father, so that our planet may be what he desired and correspond with his plan for peace, beauty and fullness (53).

What emotional response do these words strike in me? I speak with the Lord about them.

Ask for Light

Nature is a magnificent book in which God speaks to me and grants me a glimpse of his infinite beauty and goodness (12).

But the harmony between the Creator, humanity and creation is disrupted by my presuming to take the place of God and refusing to acknowledge my creaturely limitations (66).

I ask the Lord to show me how I tend to usurp the place of God and distort things so badly. What does he say in reply?

Learn where sin lies

He says:

Sister Earth now cries out to you because of the harm you have inflicted on her (2).

If you scan the regions of the planet, you see that humanity has disappointed God's expectations (61).

Because of humankind, thousands of species will no longer give glory to God by their very existence, nor convey their message to you (33).

You have not heard the cry of the earth nor the cry of the poor (49).

Confused and ashamed, I ask the Lord's forgiveness, and allow him to speak his mercy to me.

Ask, 'What Ought I Do?'

He tells me simply:

Replace greed with generosity, wastefulness with a spirit of sharing. Learn to give, and not simply to give up. This is a way of loving, of moving gradually away from what you want to what God's world needs (9).

I live in a world that is generous to me, so I ask a generous God for generosity of heart and sensitivity in my buying, my eating, my use of water and all my other choices, so that I may be reconciled with the poor and with creation.

Ask for Hope

I can cooperate as an instrument of God for the care of creation according to M own experience and talents (14).

Believing that God is present throughout creation and is always working for my good, I offer my heart for loving service. Surely the Lord responds with joy and thanks!

A Mysticism Of Service

Pope Francis is a Jesuit, so it is not surprising that his spirituality is Ignatian. This spirituality has been called a mysticism of service – union with God through loving availability for service of whatever kind. When any issue arises, St Ignatius would have us ask 'What ought I do?' He had no grandiose project for saving the world: his simple desire was, as he says, 'to help others', and he would add that 'love is found in deeds rather than in words'. He saw his life in terms of mission – being sent by God from one situation to another. He tried never to 'do his own thing' but allowed himself to be led by another.

St Ignatius refers to God labouring in the world. At one point in his life he was given profound mystical insights into how this happens, such that they made him feel as if he were 'another man with another mind'. This mystical experience brought about a reorientation of his personality and his values. From then on he saw that the love that should move him to do one thing or another must come down 'from above'. He engaged in the reform of a Rome that was Christian only in name and wrote some 7,000 letters which attest to the innumerable ways in which he tried to do what God wanted. 'Contemplative in action' describes that stance, because Ignatian spirituality is built on the art of discernment, whereby one can distinguish motivations that come from the good Spirit from those that come from other sources. Pope Francis wants the Christian community to work in this way.

This mysticism of service encompasses resistance to what is unjust. It is prophetic, and this can bring conflict, suffering and even death. The paschal mystery plays itself out in us as it did in Jesus' life. Transformative action on behalf of the kingdom of God is demanding. Work for ecological justice can make you aware that many powerful people are against you. You can remain committed to the challenges of *Laudato Si'* only through a mystical bondedness with Jesus and in solidarity with those of other faiths and none.

The Pope says:

> May our struggles and our concern for this planet never take away the joy of our hope (244).
>
> God, who calls us to generous commitment and to give him our all, offers us the light and the strength needed to continue on our way. In the heart of this world, the Lord of life, who loves us so much, is always present. He does not abandon us, for he has united himself definitively to our earth, and his love constantly impels us to find new ways forward (245).

30

The World To Come

How will it all end? Will the cosmos disappear in a puff of dust? Will the earth freeze or fry, leaving nothing behind but the darkness and silence of death? Is the story of creation no more than a cynical show conjured up by a playful deity? We know that life on earth will fade out in less than five billion years: will the cosmos roll on regardless of the loss of a tiny speck which we call planet earth, our common home?

Christian tradition on the final state of the cosmos rests on the hints given in Scripture. These hints are humble efforts to describe what is essentially beyond our understanding: we have still such little knowledge of our own planet, tiny as it is, and our knowledge of the cosmos is negligible. More than that, Isaiah tells us, and we know from experience that it's true, that the Lord of history is the God of surprises. 'I am about to do a new thing, and my thoughts are not your thoughts, nor are your ways my ways. For as the heavens are higher than the earth, so are my ways higher than your ways and my thoughts than your thoughts' (Isa 43:19) & (Isa 55:8–9).

With that firmly in mind we can 'gather the fragments, lest any be lost'. The theme of the divinisation of creation has already been noted in reference to the cosmic significance of the Eucharist. Everything created – human but also all our fellow-species and all matter – will be transfigured and re-vealed in its full glory. Even our pets will be included, surely! What we think of as irrevocably lost will be restored to its full magnificence. C S Lewis suggests that the gift of memory will act as a kind of warehouse of past reality, so that for example we will be able to revisit the fields of our childhood, though they have long been built on. Beyond the shadowlands, what is dead will come to life again, what was lost will be found. Every leaf that ever was at any time will be alive, because for God everything is now. And so for us and for all else. The Pope says:

> At the end, we will find ourselves face to face with the infinite beauty of God and will be able to read with admiration and happiness the mystery of the universe (242).

Exploring together the mystery of the universe will keep us busy and happy! But there is yet more…

31

Glorious Fulfilment

Radiant and omnipresent in this new heaven and earth, God will be revealed as infinite beauty. This God who has made us beautiful will heal our woundedness and gently wipe away our sorrow. God has always loved us but whereas here and now that is often a matter of blind faith, then we shall know it fully and be suitably overwhelmed. God's forgiveness will transform all our relationships into pure joy: there will be one ecstatic community of all creation. The labour of God on our behalf will be revealed as infinitely worthwhile. The achievement of the three divine Persons, against all the odds, in bringing all things back to their original common home, will be an unending marvel to us. The Pope says:

> Eternal life will be a shared experience of awe, in which each creature, resplendently transfigured, will take its rightful place (242).

In our resurrected flesh we shall see God, and our weary and perhaps wasted bodies will experience boundless joy and vitality. Fully alive, we shall be unrestricted in our loving, and so become like God. The despised of the earth will be revealed in their glory, and all will rejoice with surprise over their contribution to the success of the great drama of creation. We will see how divine providence interwove our joys and sufferings, our failures as well as our successes, our wrong-doings and malice, into the final story. Sin, evil and death, which ravage our world now, will be transfigured by divine light.

'All will be well, and we shall see that all will be well.' We shall indeed have eternal rest but it will be like God's rest after creating the world! God is infinite energy, so for God, resting means enjoying to the full all that is good. So we will dance, feast and play together forever and explore with God a transfigured universe. Pearse's poem with which we began concludes with the lines 'these things will pass and change, will die and be no more, and I have gone upon my way, sorrowful'. But this sorrow will be forgotten when we see all restored.

We need audacious imagination to grapple both with the challenges to our planet and with the mystery of God's infinite power to achieve 'the restoration of all things' (Acts 3:21). This divine work is already under way, so let us ask for the wisdom and audacity we need need to collaborate with God in its achievement. Amen!

POSTSCRIPT

Now that we have ended these reflections we may ask, 'Where to from here?' The answer, I believe, is that more, endlessly more, yet awaits us. Jesus says, 'To those who already have, more will be given'. We have come a long journey, and as our mystic eyes become more fully attuned, less effort is needed to trigger our awareness of the interconnectedness of all things and their links with the divine. St Ignatius of Loyola, who wasn't one to boast, acknowledged that in his later years he was 'always growing in his capacity to find God. Every time and hour he wanted to find God, he found him'. So it's possible! The contemplation of nature deepens our intuition of the presence of God in everything, and there grows in us an ever-deepening sense of the inner harmony of things.

Laudato Si' emphasises that Jesus lived in full harmony with creation (98): over and over he says to his disciples 'Look! Behold!' 'He was able to invite others to be attentive to the beauty of nature because he himself lent it an attention full of fondness and wonder' (97). We become like him in this. And because he is now the risen and glorious Lord of all creation, sthe creatures of this world no longer appear to us merely under their natural guise, because the risen One is mysteriously holding them to himself and directing them towards their fullness. The very flowers of the field and the birds which his human eyes contemplated and admired are now imbued with his radiant presence (100) and 'they carry the seed of a definitive transformation' (235). We are invited to explore this enchanted world. 'The ideal is not only to pass from the exterior to the interior to discover the action of God in the soul, but also to discover God in all things' (233). Some writers affirm that we are entering the mystical age, that we are all mystics, and that the mystic heart – the deepest part of who we are – is beginning to awaken. *Laudato Si'* has opened the door for us to find God in the tiniest things as well as the most awesome. The mystic experiences the intimate connection between God and all beings (234).

An incident while I was writing this book has unexpectedly brought me to a deeper perception of tiny things. I used to love to roam the Wicklow hills, enjoying the wide landscape and sky in a general way. One day I returned to my car to find the windows shattered, and to avoid a recurrence of this disaster I decided that in future I would have to park in a safe place near a café. My walks have become very repetitive as a result, but they have brought me to focus on small familiar things along the roadside – flowers, mosses, running water, brambles, gorse, dead vegetation, weathered granite, ageing trees, leaves in abundance, scurrying ants, birdsong… None of these is remarkable, but I'm learning that each has its own unique life story, and I am beginning to listen. I see that Darwin was right to say that 'it is interesting to contemplate an entangled bank…' and I've been forced by circumstances to accept his invitation. We share existence with all other species in a universe which is sacred because the Spirit plays in it and everything I observe is expressing divine energy. 'Nature not only points to God but is itself the place of God's presence' (88). With Jacob lying on his pillow of stone I can say of my little hedgerows, 'Surely God is in this place, and I did not know it. How awesome it is: this is none other than the house of God; this is the gate of heaven!' (Gen 28:16–17). The divinisation both of ourselves and of the world we love is well underway, and with mystic eyes we can intuit it and enter its harmony!

Let us conclude with the Pope's message of hope:

> The Spirit of God fills the universe with possibilities, and therefore from the heart of things, something new can always emerge (80).

> The God who created the universe out of nothing can also intervene in this world and overcome every form of evil (74).

> May our struggles and our concern for this planet never take away the joy of our hope (244).

Let this conviction give us the energy and imagination we need to restore to its intended beauty our common home.

Further Reading

An immense bibliography is building up around the themes of *Laudato Si*. Among many authors, I am particularly indebted to the following for help on my own journey: Una Agnew: *The Mystical Imagination of Patrick Kavanagh: A Buttonhole in Heaven?* 1998; Luke Bell OSB: *The Meaning of Blue: Recovering a Contemplative Spirit*, 2014; Margaret Daly-Denton: *John: An Earth Bible Commentary: Supposing Him to Be the Gardener*, 2017; Elizabeth A Johnson: *Ask the Beasts: Darwin and the God of Love*, 2014; Sean McDonagh: *On Care for Our Common Home: Laudato Si'*, 2016, and *Laudato Si': An Irish Response*, 2017; John O'Donohue: *Divine Beauty*, 2003; Diarmuid O Murchu: *Incarnation*, 2017; Carlo Rovelli: *Seven Brief Letters on Physics*, 2015; *Reality is Not What It Seems*, 2017, and Teilhard de Chardin: *The Divine Milieu*, 1961. Finally my thanks to innumerable poets who have articulated so beautifully how the Holy meets us when it chooses, in one or other of creation's disguises; as Patrick Kavanagh says, 'I have a belief in poetry as a mystical thing'.